FRACTIONS IN DISGUISE

PROPERTY OF
George Cornelius Factor

A Math Adventure by
Edward Einhorn

Illustrated by
David Clark

ini Charlesbridge

To my niece Diana Hallie: you may be only ⅕ my size right now, but you fill more than a fraction of my heart—E. E.

Published by Charlesbridge
85 Main Street
Watertown, MA 02472
(617) 926-0329
www.charlesbridge.com

Library of Congress Cataloging-in-Publication Data
Einhorn, Edward (Edward Arthur), 1970–
    Fractions in disguise : a math adventure / Edward Einhorn ; illustrated by David Clark.
        p. cm.
    Audience: 7–10.
    ISBN 978-1-57091-773-8 (reinforced for library use)
    ISBN 978-1-57091-774-5 (softcover)
    ISBN 978-1-60734-604-3 (ebook)
1. Fractions—Juvenile literature. I. Clark, David, 1960 Mar. 19– II. Title.
QA117.E36 2013
513.2'6—dc23   2012024435

Printed in Singapore
(hc) 10 9 8 7 6 5 4 3 2 1
(sc) 10 9 8 7 6 5 4 3 2 1

Illustrations done in ink and watercolor
Display type and text type set in Birch Standard by Adobe and ITC Berkeley Oldstyle
Color separations by KHL Chroma Graphics, Singapore
Printed and bound September 2013 by Imago in Singapore
Production supervision by Brian G. Walker
Designed by Martha MacLeod Sikkema

Some kids collect baseball cards. Some collect action figures. Me? I collect fractions. I've been collecting them for exactly ⅔ of my life. In my bedroom, shelves full of fractions cover ¾ of the walls.

Maybe it's because I was born during a half moon. Or maybe it's because I'm ¼ genius, ¼ stubborn, ⅓ determined, and ⅙ crazy. But for me, it all adds up to one thing: I can't get enough of those darn fractions.

So when a brand-new $\frac{5}{9}$ went up for auction, you know I was first in line to buy it. The $\frac{5}{9}$ is a thing of beauty. When you first look at it, it looks like a $\frac{1}{2}$, but the more you look, the more you realize it's just a little bit more.

The room was filled with the regular customers: Baron von Mathematik, Madame de Géométrique, and the mysterious Dr. Brok, a former university professor rumored to have been fired for the illegal possession of a $\frac{4}{0}$.

I bid $\frac{1}{2}$ of a million dollars. Madame de Géométrique bid $\frac{3}{4}$ of a million. Baron von Mathematik bid $\frac{7}{8}$ of a million. Our bids were clearly approaching one million dollars. Would we ever reach it?

5

Suddenly we found ourselves in darkness. "There's foul play afoot!" cried the baron.

His fears proved true. When the lights went back on, the $\frac{5}{9}$ was nowhere to be seen. Neither was Dr. Brok.

"Alas, he's stolen it!" exclaimed Baron von Mathematik.

"He never gets his fractions fair and square," agreed Madame de Géométrique.

"But how can he hope to hide it?" I asked.

"He is a master of disguise, Mr. Factor," Madame de Géométrique explained. "He can take a $\frac{1}{2}$ and turn it into a $\frac{2}{4}$ or a $\frac{3}{6}$. It's still the same fraction, but it looks different."

"So am I to understand that he could take a $\frac{3}{5}$ . . . ," I began.

". . . multiply the 3 by 4 and the 5 by 4 . . . ," continued Madame de Géométrique.

". . . and have something that looks like a $\frac{12}{20}$?" I concluded.

"But it's still $\frac{3}{5}$ really," Madame de Géométrique agreed. "He just doesn't want you to know it."

"My poor, beautiful fraction!" wailed Baron von Mathematik.

"Don't despair," I said. "I have an idea."

That night I worked till dawn. By morning I had what I needed: a Reducer.

What is a Reducer? It's ½ ray gun and ½ calculator, made from a whole lot of paper clips, a whisk, some discarded computer parts, and sheer ingenuity. What does it do? It removes the disguise from a fraction and reduces it to its lowest terms.

I tested it out that morning. For a long time I had owned a $^{10}/_{15}$, but I suspected that it could be another fraction in disguise.

I pointed the Reducer at it and dialed a 2. The top number (or numerator, as we call it in the trade) wavered, trying to turn into a 5, but the bottom number (or denominator) stayed the same. I dialed a 3, and the denominator tried to transform into a 5, but the numerator wouldn't budge. I dialed a 4, and nothing happened. Finally, I dialed a 5.

The fraction changed completely. The 10 became a 2 and the 15 became a 3, leaving me with a sleek $^{2}/_{3}$. The Reducer was ready to go.

Dr. Brok lived in a mansion that had to be $\frac{1}{10}$ of a mile tall. When I rang the bell, he opened the door halfway.

"Let me in, Doctor," I told him. "I know you have the $\frac{5}{9}$ in there, and I'm going to find it."

"Come in, come in," he purred. "Take a look around. You'll see no $\frac{5}{9}$ in here."

I went in. There were fractions everywhere—piled on shelves, bursting from cupboards, covering the floor. There was even an enormous $^{100}/_{100}$ hanging from the ceiling.

Quickly I spotted my first fraud. "That $^{3}/_{21}$," I said. "It's really a $^{1}/_{7}$, isn't it?" I pointed my Reducer at the fraction and dialed a 3. Both the numerator and the denominator were divided, and now I had a $^{1}/_{7}$ before me, as I had suspected.

"That's a very . . . interesting device you have there," commented Dr. Brok, eyeing the Reducer nervously. "Ingenious, really."

$$\frac{3}{21} \div \frac{3}{3} = \frac{1}{7}$$

I spotted another suspicious fraction. Could that be the $\frac{5}{9}$ in disguise? It was a $\frac{34}{63}$, and it looked familiar. I dialed a 2, 3, 4, 5, 6, 7 . . . Nothing seemed to work.

"You can't reduce that one," said Dr. Brok. "That fraction's already reduced to its lowest terms, I'm afraid."

He was smiling in secret satisfaction as he said it, but he was right. That fraction was as reduced as it could be.

I found a few more fractions that could be reduced—an $8/10$ became a $4/5$, a $2/16$ became a $1/8$, and an $11/22$ became a $1/2$—but no $5/9$.

I even looked through the garbage, full of old fractions and fraction pieces so small they were worthless. I found a piece from a $1/28$, a $1/63$, and a $1/92$. The $5/9$ was nowhere to be seen. There was something I was missing . . .

"Well, it was nice of you to visit," Dr. Brok began saying. "I would invite you to stay longer, but I was just about to polish all my frac—"

"This $1/63$—where did it come from?" I interrupted.

"It's just an old, broken fraction," sputtered Dr. Brok.

21

Quickly I raced back to the $^{34}/_{63}$. The tiny $^{1}/_{63}$ fit perfectly into it, making the fraction a $^{35}/_{63}$. This was a fraction that could be reduced!

"Wait, no!" cried Dr. Brok.

34/63

But it was too late. I had already pointed the Reducer and dialed a 7. The 35 divided and became a 5, while the 63 divided and became a 9. There it was, right in front of me: the ⁵⁄₉ I had been looking for.

"Very clever," Dr. Brok said with a sneer. "I didn't think you had it in you."

He raced up the stairs and unhooked a rope. Suddenly the $^{100}/_{100}$ above me began falling, all one hundred pieces of it looking like daggers. I dialed the Reducer up to 100, aimed high, and jumped for cover.

A solid disc landed with a clatter and rolled away. The $^{100}/_{100}$ had become a single whole, no longer a fraction at all. But Dr. Brok was gone.

Baron von Mathematik and Madame de Géométrique couldn't believe it when I told them the story.

"You did it, Mr. Factor!" the baron cried, saluting me.

"The fraction is yours," said Madame de Géométrique. "You earned it."

I put it in the most prominent place on my top shelf, right next to the Reducer. Now, every morning, when dawn comes, the first ray of light through my window lands right on the $\frac{5}{9}$.

It doesn't look half bad.

REDUCING FRACTIONS

Simple—that's the biggest little word in the fraction game. The simpler the fraction, the easier it is to add or subtract. In mathspeak, the Reducer works by finding the greatest common factor (GCF), the largest number that both the numerator and the denominator can be divided by.

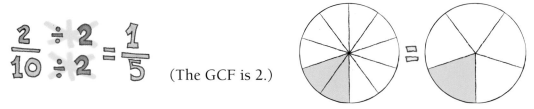

$$\frac{2 \div 2}{10 \div 2} = \frac{1}{5}$$ (The GCF is 2.)

This makes it easier to find the lowest common denominator (LCD), the smallest number that the denominator can be, while keeping in mind that the denominator needs to be the same in all fractions when you add or subtract them.

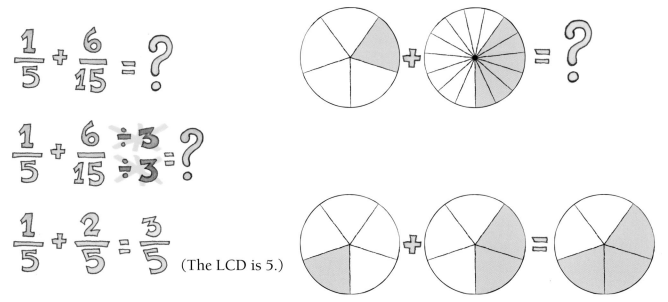

$$\frac{1}{5} + \frac{6}{15} = ?$$

$$\frac{1}{5} + \frac{6 \div 3}{15 \div 3} = ?$$

$$\frac{1}{5} + \frac{2}{5} = \frac{3}{5}$$ (The LCD is 5.)

As any fraction collector will tell you, reducing a fraction can be very handy. And who knows? It may be a very valuable fraction—in disguise!